Mindful
SPACES

MINDFULNESS AND NATURE

Written by Dr Rhianna Watts and Katie Woolley
Illustrated by Sarah Jennings

WAYLAND

Franklin Watts
First published in Great Britain in 2022 by Wayland

Credits
Series Editor: Sarah Peutrill
Series Designer: Lisa Peacock

HB ISBN: 978 1 5263 2102 2
PB ISBN: 978 1 5263 2103 9

Printed in China

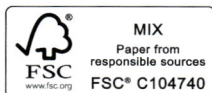

FSC
www.fsc.org
MIX
Paper from
responsible sources
FSC® C104740

Wayland, an imprint of
Hachette Children's Group
Part of Hodder and Stoughton
Carmelite House
50 Victoria Embankment
London EC4Y 0DZ

An Hachette UK Company
www.hachette.co.uk
www.hachettechildrens.co.uk

SAFETY PRECAUTIONS

We recommend adult supervision at all times while doing the exercises and activities in this book, particularly outdoors and activities involving exercise, glue and cutting. When you are doing creative activities:

- Cover surfaces.
- Tie back long hair.
- Ask an adult for help with cutting.
- Check all ingredients for allergens.

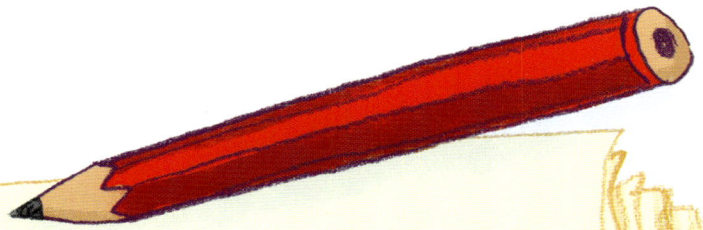

Contents

WHAT IS MINDFULNESS?

Mindfulness is the practice of paying attention to what is happening inside your mind and your body right now, as well as what is happening in the world around you.

Nature is an important part of mindfulness. Paying attention to the world, the places you go and the things you see, hear, smell, touch and taste can help you become more mindful.

Forest Bathing

The Buddha was a man who live thousands of years ago. One day, he found a deep sense of peace while he meditated under a tree. Forest bathing or *shinrin-yoku* is a Japanese process of relaxation. It is all about listening to the calm and quiet as you walk through the trees, just like the Buddha once did. Why not give it a go? Take a walk through the woods, breathing in and out deeply as you look at nature all around you.

HOW THIS ACTIVITY HELPS

Regularly spending time outside helps you feel calmer and happier. You can concentrate better and be more creative. It also helps your body be strong and healthy.

MINDFULNESS TODAY

Today, people practise mindfulness to help them feel good in their minds and their bodies. Mindfulness teaches you to slow down and notice your thoughts and emotions as they happen, without getting caught up in them.

As you notice your body and the way it responds to the world around you, you can start to enjoy more positive experiences that you might have missed before.

The sand is so soft.

The air tastes salty.

I like this pretty starfish.

Treasure Hunt

Go on a treasure hunt in your favourite outdoor spot. Can you find an object to match each of these statements?

something soft ☑

something hard ☑

something green ☑

something rough ☑

something round ☑

something smooth ☑

something long ☑

something you find beautiful ☑

HOW THIS ACTIVITY HELPS

By making a choice to slow down and explore the natural world, you can begin to appreciate all it has to offer.

NATURE'S CHANGES

Nature is always moving. Weather rolls in and rolls out again, shoots that start to sprout in spring take root deep in the soil, slowly growing into trees over many seasons. Animals undergo beautiful transformations day in, day out.

Just like nature, we are always changing, too. What is happening around us changes moment by moment, and so do our thoughts and emotions. Slowing down and paying closer attention to nature's ever-changing beauty helps us live in the here and now and listen to our minds and our bodies as they change and grow.

Cloud Gazing

Lie on a patch of grass and watch the clouds roll by. Notice how the clouds move and change. Pick a cloud in the sky, and breathe in and out slowly as you watch and wait for it to disappear.

HOW THIS EXERCISE HELPS

Taking the time to watch nature come and go can help you learn to notice changes in your own thoughts and emotions.

SEEING THE WORLD ANEW

When you practise mindfulness, you may start to notice new things and become more curious about nature as you feel more connected to the natural world. Being open to the world around you, can make you want to find out about it, as you ask lots of interesting questions!

Why can we see the night's stars more clearly in the countryside than in a town?

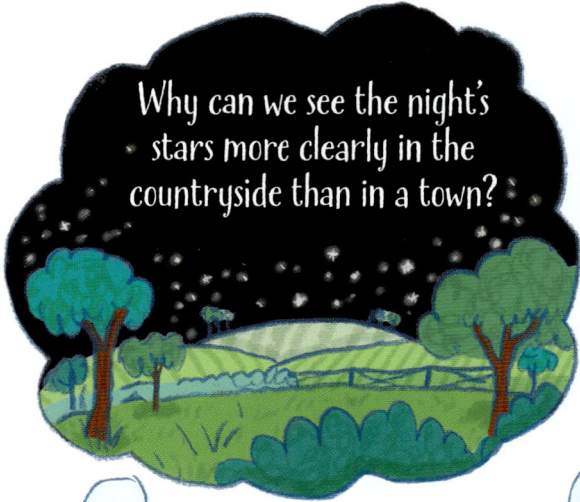

How much nectar does a bee collect every day?

Why do the ocean's waves ebb and flow with the pull of the Moon?

Mindfulness helps you look beyond yourself and think about the world around you. It opens you up to being curious about Earth's wildlife and its habitats, how other people live and how you can take care of nature.

Activity

Nature's Frame

Create a picture frame to help you be more curious about the wonder of nature all around you. You will need: a piece of card, a pencil, some scissors and colouring pens or pencils.

1. Draw a rectangle on a piece of card. Then draw a bigger one, 2 cm outside the first one, so that there is a smaller shape within a larger one.
2. Cut out the middle of the small rectangle to make a picture frame.
3. You can decorate your frame if you wish.
4. Take your frame outside and hold it up to nature all around you. What can you see through your frame? What pictures can you take?

HOW THIS ACTIVITY HELPS

Focusing on nature through a frame asks you to look at something in a new way and helps you spot new things when you do.

A BREATH OF FRESH AIR

Life is busy. You often need to rush about and the world sometimes seems to be rushing around you. You can get caught up in its busyness, and it can feel like you are in the middle of a storm being blown about by the wind.

Breathing in fresh air as you pay attention to your breath and how it feels in your body can anchor your thoughts and your emotions. This helps you feel calmer when life gets too busy.

My Anchored Breath

* Stand outside with your feet slightly apart and your body tall and proud. If you can, close your eyes and pay attention to your breath as you breathe in through your nose. Notice what it feels like as it enters your nostrils and fills your chest.

* Breathe out through your mouth. Notice what it feels like as the air empties from your chest and leaves your mouth. Spend a few moments doing this.

* Now, widen your attention to the things you can hear and feel around you. Notice the wind on your body. Is it cold or warm? Listen to the sounds of nature: birds singing, trees rustling and the wind blowing across your skin. Spend a few moments doing this.

* Bring your attention back to your breath.

* When you are ready, open your eyes. As you go about your day, if you feel like you are becoming anxious or worried, take a few moments to pause and connect with your breath and the nature around you.

HOW THIS EXERCISE HELPS

Paying attention to your breath can help calm your mind and your body during difficult moments.

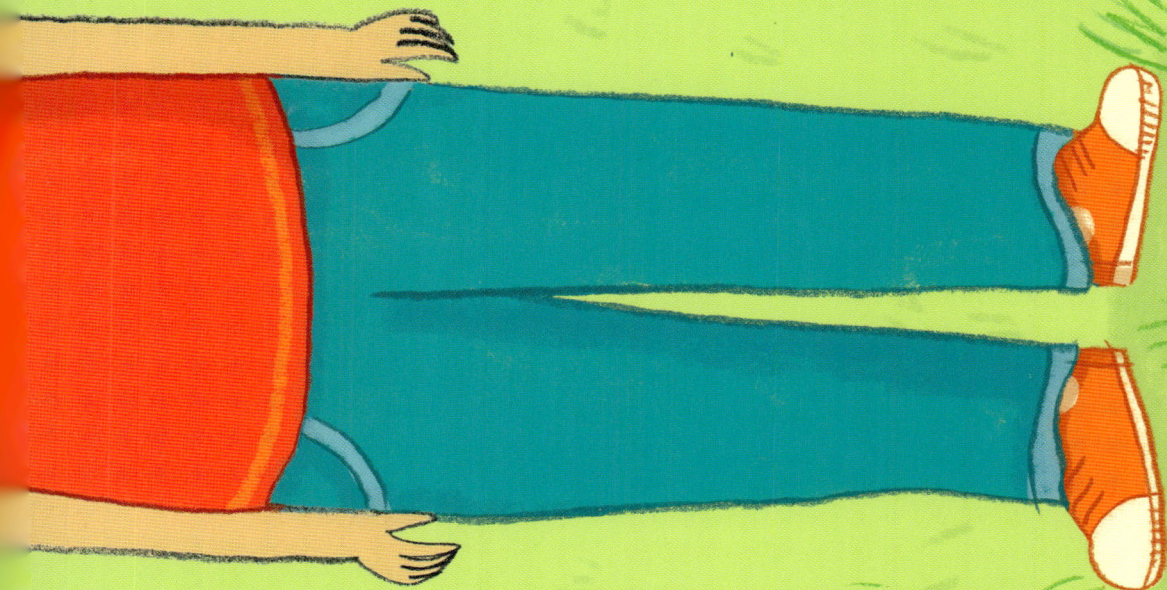

YOUR MIND, YOUR SENSES

Mindfulness is a skill and, like all skills, it requires practice. The more you practise, the easier it becomes – a bit like exercising your physical muscles and building muscle memory in your body.

You can practise mindfulness in nature anywhere. It doesn't have to be a 'natural' environment, such as the beach or a forest. If you use your senses (touch, taste, sight, smell and hearing) you can experience nature anywhere. This awareness helps you focus on, and enjoy, the present moment more easily.

Lift up a small rock and see what's underneath.

Look at the flowers in bloom.

Notice the insects buzzing about and the birds flitting past houses and buildings.

Kneel down and feel the ground under your hands.

Explore Your Senses

Grab some binoculars and head out into the great outdoors. As you walk mindfully, stop every so often and look all around you. What can you see? What can you hear? What can you smell? What can you touch?

HOW THIS EXERCISE HELPS

It is hard to be caught up in the past or the future when you are paying attention to what your senses are telling you about your present experience.

NATURE'S COLOURS

Your sight is a powerful mindfulness tool. As you watch and notice nature all around you, you start to slow down and be aware of how it makes you think and feel.

Nature is full of colours, shapes and patterns. Mindfulness can help you begin to spot nature's beauty. What colour are the first flowers of spring? How many circles can you see on your walk to school? Find a bird's feather (but don't pick it up). What patterns cover it?

Mindful Colouring

Colouring can help you focus your mind on the present moment. It is relaxing and good fun to draw and colour pictures of nature in a mindful way.

* Take a pad of paper and green pens or pencils. Try to find as many different shades of green as possible!
* Look for green things outside, for example trees, grass, leaves or insects.
* What different shades of green do you see?
* Have a go at drawing an object or a scene using your green colouring pens. Don't worry about making it look perfect. Instead, focus on drawing all the various shades of green and how they look together.

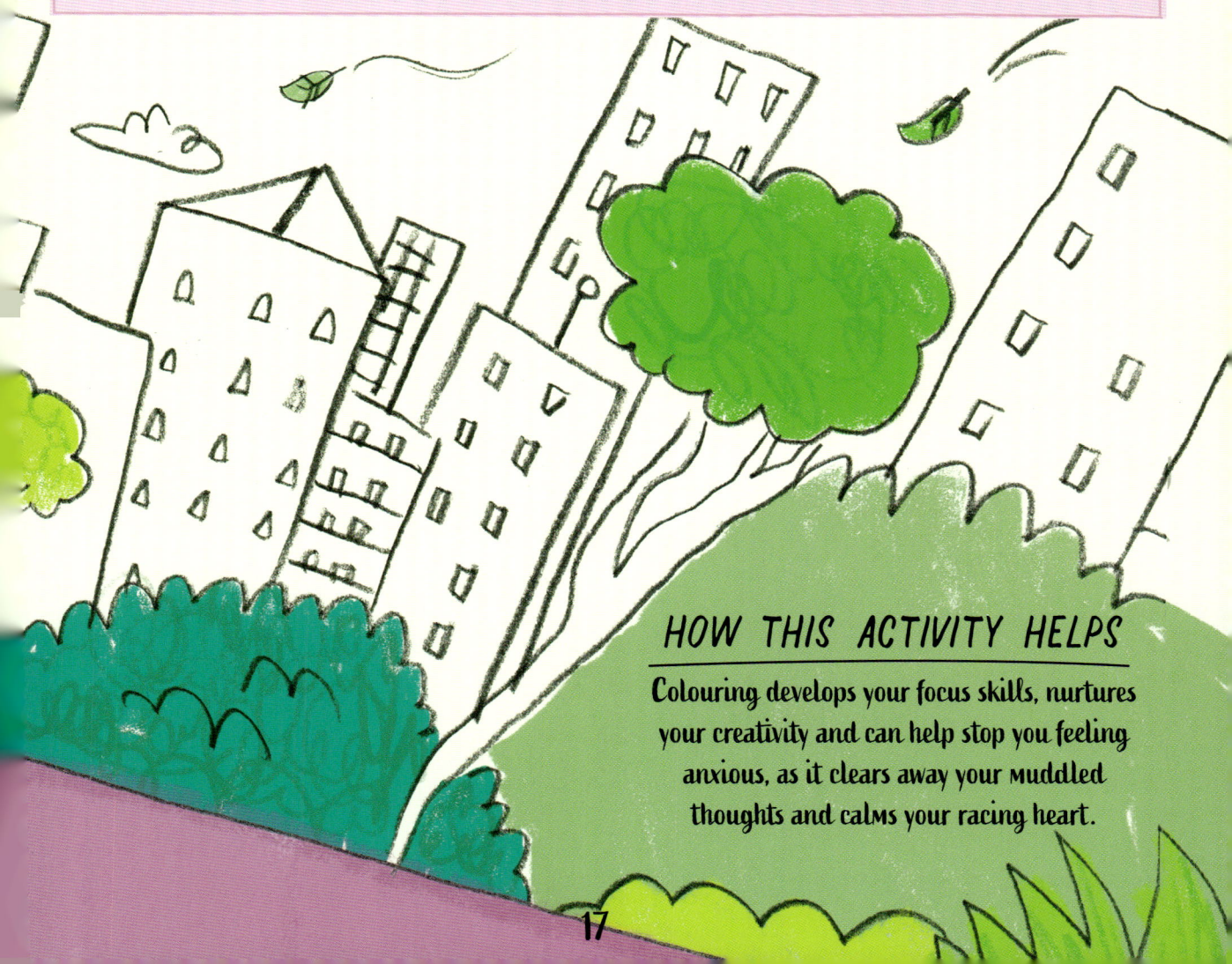

HOW THIS ACTIVITY HELPS

Colouring develops your focus skills, nurtures your creativity and can help stop you feeling anxious, as it clears away your muddled thoughts and calms your racing heart.

NATURE'S TREASURES

Like sight, your sense of touch is a powerful tool, too.
Paying close attention to all the things that you can touch
outside connects you to the present moment.

Nature is full of all sorts of physical
sensations. For example, the wind blows
across your skin and through your hair,
the grass tickles your toes and the
bark of a tree trunk is rough to touch,
while a flower's petals are soft and silky.
Mindfulness helps you become more aware
of these sensations as you enjoy them.

A Nature Bag

Take a bag with you on your next walk. When you are outside, look for objects that will help you feel connected to the world around you. Remember to ask an adult if an object is safe to collect before you pick it up. When you are back at home, close your eyes and explore the treasures inside your bag. Notice how each object feels, and what thoughts, emotions and memories come up as you hold each one.

HOW THIS ACTIVITY HELPS

A nature bag is a good way to remain connected to nature once you are back inside. It can help you relax as you remember the happy thoughts and feelings you felt when you were outside.

REMEMBER!

Always check with a grown-up that you can take home any treasures you find on your adventures. You shouldn't take pebbles from a beach or wild flowers from a meadow, for example, as it can harm the environment.

NATURE'S PATTERNS

As you become more mindful of the natural world around you, you will start to notice patterns and cycles in nature. Just think about the changes nature goes through in one day! Over one year nature's seasons change, and animals and plants are born, grow, reproduce and die. Nature moves in circles or cycles.

Being mindful when you go outside will help you notice nature's patterns. It may also help you start to notice patterns in your own thoughts, emotions and actions as you use mindfulness to pay more attention to them. By noticing patterns and changes, you can decide if they are helpful or not, and whether you want to let the pattern carry on or try to change it.

Create a Sundial

Observe the Sun's movements over the hours in a day. You will need: a sunny day, a stick, some playdough, a white piece of paper and a pencil.

1. Place the playdough in the middle of the bottom of your paper.
2. Push your stick into the playdough so that it stands upright.
3. Outside in the sunshine, mark the position of your stick's shadow every hour during the day.
4. Notice the way the shadow moves as the Sun travels across the sky.

HOW THIS ACTIVITY HELPS

Slowing down and noticing patterns and cycles outside can help you connect with nature.

NATURE'S JOURNEY

The patterns and cycles of nature cannot be hurried or rushed.
They happen when the time is right and not a moment before.

Nature is on its own journey and mindfulness can help you
appreciate it, while giving you tools to slow down and
pay closer attention to your own life.

Rather than becoming caught up in wishes for the future, you can use
mindfulness to learn to take delight in the moment, as nature does,
rather than become too caught up in your final destination.

Mindful Movements

When you next go outside, put your arms out wide and slowly begin to turn round and round.

* Notice what it feels like in your body to twirl.
* What does the air feel like as it whooshes around your body?
* What emotions arise? What thoughts come into your mind?
* Then, refocus your mind back to the action of twirling and spend a few moments placing all of your attention on simply moving.

HOW THIS EXERCISE HELPS

This exercise practises focus. Sometimes you can get so caught up in your thoughts that you forget to be present. It can be helpful to simply practise 'doing'.

NATURE'S SEEDS

Nature is full of new beginnings. Seeds grow into flowers or plants. Eggs hatch and grow into birds. Slowing down and noticing these new beginnings, then watching them flourish over time, develops skills of patience and a deep connection to the natural world around you.

You don't need a garden, or indeed any outside space of your own, to connect mindfully with nature. Simply growing plants on a window sill or bird watching from your window is a good way to mindfully appreciate the nature around you.

Activity

Grow Your Own Cress

Choosing to spend time planting seeds helps you practise many of the values that are important to mindfulness.

1. **Firstly, you need to focus on the task.**
   Carefully put compost into a pot and add your cress seeds. It's OK if your mind wanders but try and bring it back to the activity.

2. Don't forget to water your seeds.

3. Place your cress seeds in a sunny spot on your windowsill.

4. **Secondly, you must be patient.** Plants take time to put down roots and send up shoots. Pay attention to your cress seeds every day. How many days do you have to wait before you see a little green shoot?

5. **Finally, you must not give up.** You will need to water your plants regularly (but not too much).

HOW THIS ACTIVITY HELPS

By slowing down, noticing and watching, you can develop patience and a better connection to the world around you.

MOTHER EARTH

We all need nature to live. We need trees to breathe, we need plants to eat and we need to drink water everyday. We enjoy nature's delights, such as honey from the honeybee.

Mindfulness means you become more aware of nature and its riches. Taking the time to learn about how food is grown and where it comes from, while being mindful about how you eat it, helps you appreciate your place on Earth and how nature looks after your body.

Where Food Comes From

When you sit down to eat your next meal, pause to think about all the people involved in the creation of the food in front of you.

1. Someone planted seeds and helped them grow.

2. Someone harvested the food at the right time of year.

4. Someone prepared the food for you to eat.

3. Someone filled the shelves in the shop.

HOW THIS EXERCISE HELPS

Slowing down to think about all these people makes it impossible not to be grateful for all their hard work.

NATURE'S ADVENTURES

Today, people spend a lot of time inside, using electronic devices, like smartphones, tablets or computers to do school learning, to work and to connect with friends and family. Practising mindfulness when you do go outside can help you have a digital detox and reconnect with your natural world.

Putting down your device and heading outside to do these mindful activities will help you reconnect with the world around you.

Tree pose

Activity

Tell a Story

Tell a story on your walk and include some yoga poses as you pause to enjoy the outside world.

"One day, two friends went for a walk in the woods ...

They came across a rock covered with moss ...

Rock pose

From behind the green rock,
out slithered a hissing snake ...

The children were scared. They ran away and
clambered up a huge mountain to safety."

Cobra pose

Mountain pose

Activity

Bird Spotting

On a walk near your home, keep a tally of the birds you see. Can you name any of them? Do you recognise their bird calls? Take a pair of binoculars with you if you'd like to see your feathery friends up close. You'll need to be still, calm and quiet. Look all around you, in the sky, up in the trees and on the ground, too.

MINDFULNESS TIPS

Mindfulness helps anchor you in the present moment. It helps you feel confident and ready to tackle the day. It can help you navigate big emotions, and it can also help you find moments of calm in your busy world.

Here are some tips to help you practise mindfulness.

* You can practise mindfulness anywhere and at any time. Mindfulness simply means choosing to pay attention to what is happening inside your mind and body, and what is happening around you, in the present moment, right here and right now.

* You can do this by sitting and focusing on your breath for five minutes in bed before you go to sleep, or you could do this by focusing on what you can see and hear whilst walking to school!

* Your breath and how it feels in your body is very important. Paying attention to your breath helps you to focus on what is happening in the present moment. Your breath is like an anchor for your mind and body. It can stop them floating away.

* It's okay if you start to feel a bit bored or if your mind wanders. If you can, just notice this and refocus your mind to where you want it to be. If you get stuck, be kind to yourself. Remember you are learning a new skill, and you can always try again another day.

* If your body starts to feel uncomfortable, notice where in your body you feel any aches and move so you are in a more comfortable position. However, always stop doing an exercise if you feel pain.

INDEX

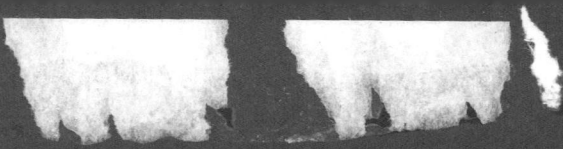